A Bank Robber's Bad Luck With His Ex-Girlfriend

KJ Hannah Greenberg

ISBN 978-1-936373-22-2

©2011 KJ Hannah Greenberg. All rights reserved. No part of this publication may be reproduced or transmitted in any form or by any means, electronic or mechanical, without permission in writing from the publisher. Requests for permission to make copies of any part of this work should be e-mailed to info@unboundcontent.com.

Published in the United States by Unbound Content, LLC, Englewood, NJ.

Cover art ©2011, by KJ Hannah Greenberg.

Author photo ©2011, by Yiftach Paltrowitz

The poems in this collection are all original and previously unpublished with the exception of those listed at the credits page at the end of the volume.

A Bank Robber's Bad Luck With His Ex-Girlfriend
First edition 2011

Acknowledgments

Much credit ought to be ceded to my husband. For more than three decades that beleaguered man has remembered to kiss me before we tuck in for bed despite the fact that I write critically about relationships in general and about the male species in particular. Fortunately, whereas I rant, I also rave. Although I espouse the cynicism of the modern woman, I likewise articulate the affection of the world's history of spouses.

Table of Contents

Foreword 7
Introduction: A Bank Robber's Bad Luck With His Ex-Girlfriend 9

HOPE

A Special Dance 11
Engineering Wizards' Best and Last (Interstate Enchantment) 12
Greyhound Buses Race Love 13
Friendsake 14
Michael's Mnemonics: Restimulating RAMS *before* Finals 15
Clandestine Typewritten Message 16
Your Tongue Quicks Me 18
Fraternity Pin 19
C'est L'Amour N'est-ce Pas 20
Goldy and the Bear: A Modern *Cyrch a Chuta* for Two Brain-Fried Nerds ...21
A Midsummer *Alcaics* 22
Apple 23
A Young Co-ed's Argonaut-Inspired Springtime Fancy 24
Joining 25
Gibbous Shoats and Other of Ardor's Follies 26
My Boyfriend Coughs Up Platitudes 27

HURT

Heart's Cry Bed: Recalibrating for the New Semester 29
Goldfish Hangover 30
Trumpeters, Drummers, Dancers, plus Elephants: Princes' Promises 31
Poisoning via Toothbrush After "Romancing" 32
An *Ae Freislighe*: How to Get Your Girlfriend Pregnant 33
Graphic, Animated Features 34
Crocodile Tears 35
Christina Rossetti's "Birthday" to a Satirical Beat 36
Stained Sheets: Some Emotional Hazards of Hooking Up 37
Simple Arithmetic 38
Trees at Sunset 39
Sentiment's Chowder 40
While the Dew Coughed 41
Quinoa in My Keyboard and Other Traces of Fantasy 42
Small Payment for a Protracted Span 43
Deviating Under Starlight: Whispers of Divestment 44

HIGHWAYS

Decided 47
Colluvium 48
My Chemistry Class 49
Droving Last Year's Love 50
Fire Song 51
Ephemerids 52
Your Knees Remain Extant: Deriding an Internet Hussy 54
His Mistresses' Grandeur Astride Common Sense 55
Pausing From Eating Shelducks 56
Some Cowboys 57
Among Bungalows 58
When Lowing Wisents Agitate 59
Reciprocity 60
Three Pillows 61
Ready to Synchronize 62
Emotional Kerfuffles: Second Unions 63
Conclusion: Hurt Is to Healing 64

APPENDIX

A Birthday, by Christina Rossetti 67

About the Author 69
Publication Credits 71

Foreword

Songbirds are entertaining. Roses smell nice. Most passion, however, resolves as cacophonous and stinky. In *A Bank Robber's Bad Luck With His Ex-Girlfriend*, this mess, to which love often gets reduced, is poked at, prodded a lot, and eventually pushed over. Whereas money might buy all manners of dalliance, and fame might catapult a person past social mores, a good, strong kick, such as is offered in *A Bank Robber's Bad Luck With His Ex-Girlfriend*, can most successfully level the difference between interpersonal decency and liaisons' impropriety.

To wit, *A Bank Robber's Bad Luck With His Ex-Girlfriend* employs a mixture of contemporary and traditional forms, including *ae freislighe*, ballad, *cyrch a chuta*, and free verse, as it proffers the tang of real or imagined, but almost always piquant, romantic life. First love, serial marriages, fidelity, adultery, crushes, callous calculations, and much more are explicated in this collection's unabashed adjudication of relationships.

Concurrently tough, sassy, and hopeful, this book strives to press up against soft concepts of intimate associations. Articulated regrets, muted longings, and rudimentary joy all slide among these pages. From the initial poem, "A Bank Robber's Bad Luck With His Ex-Girlfriend," to the concluding verse, "Hurt Is to Healing," this volume gives readers images and language with which to wrestle with affection's important, awkward, and contested moments.

Whereas you might be tempted to forgo all further human experiments in favor of cloistering yourself with an imaginary hedgehog or whereas you might find it easier to pretend that all is right with your current situation than to redefine your personal boundaries, allow *A Bank Robber's Bad Luck With His Ex-Girlfriend* to help you own your volition. It might be imprudent to act otherwise.

KJ Hannah Greenberg
Jerusalem
2011

Introduction: A Bank Robber's Bad Luck With His Ex-Girlfriend

Sun-faded bookstands,
Neatly stacked, yellowed files,
Sum our common significance.

Your occasional night feedings,
Threw my axels at odd angles,
Rang my chuckwagon bell.

Yet, lambies and kids never dared
Merge their needs;
Village norms trump in the marketplace.

My small cabin meant shelter,
Not refuge; no space for bandits, here.
Fenceposts mark my ranches.

Consider, the staid, local law says
(Fiduciary institutions, aside)
Sniveling's no solace for roundups.

HOPE

A Special Dance

It could not be this special dance,
Could blind us past this special trance.
It could not seem our special pair,
Could bring us worse than we have here.
It could not be.

It will not be this call once heard,
Could bring us worse than ancient words.
It will not be this mating song,
Could leave us short, will bring us wrong.
It will not be.

So love beware, so love be warned,
There are the lows; there are the harms.
But our embrace will shield our hearts,
Will sponsor us, will prove our start.
It must be.

Engineering Wizards' Best and Last (Interstate Enchantment)

Arabic assistant's poetics,
Like Champagne bubbles' holiday tricks,
Turn little. Hours of Aristotle,
Salad friends tossed, when shared with the bottle,
Bring no strawberry-grass dreams, nor tease
Smiles from tears. Midnight movies' release
Finds telephone's magic, plus charming peace.
Receiver's as warm as achievement's past.
Engineering wizards' best and last
Spell. Word blankets soothe; their wrap holds fast.

Greyhound Buses Race Love

Eight a.m. Greyhounds race love,
Packaged. Rain drops, wet eyes, shoved
Beneath seats with umbrellas'
Vinyl greetings.

Daffodils push up past earth,
Morning visage's lush, yet unbirthed,
Fragile blossoms close;
Sunshine's distanced.

Departure creates our spaces,
Young buds learn to face
Isolation's wind, when
Springtime's harsh.

Bird calls. Baby blooms.
Hearts' rage, other rooms
Cloud feelings.
Eight a.m. Greyhounds race love.

Friendsake

Touch my hand.
Fingers mean to extend
My heart's tendrils.

Michael's Mnemonics:
Restimulating RAMS *before* Finals

Smudgy duds of thought,
Alternating with a trillion hits of
Little, fluttery, bitsy bits.
Recollection rattled, throttled, started from
A frothing styrofoam mug.

Thick, sheaf-doms encamped camel-up,
Desert stars resuscitated to
Spill, trickle, and echo. echo.
Seams of sand collapsing, dug deep by
Broken wood and lead.

Paper armies stationary, artilleries reactivated,
Standards rectified with firework thunder.
Destination parapets fortified while
Long, linear, intellectual things remobilize with
Gnawed pencils and dank coffee.

KJ Hannah Greenberg

Clandestine Typewritten Message

Sleepy like puppies,
We nuzzled together,
Covers and pillows provided.
Reflecting on duties,
We puzzled our leisure,
Grabbed clothing, each other, collided.

Tooth brushes,
Mint toothpaste,
Earrings, gold chain clasp.
A long search for contacts,
For short socks that matched.
Umbrella. Umbrella. Jackets.

Stop! CAT!

Strawberry jam and bread,
Confounded door latch.
Car keys and thrown news,
Gray engine smoke.
Traffic laws, fast lane,
Big kiss and small stroke.

Gray as September,
Wet like December,
The clouds leaked over the trees.
Soon after we parted,
Your fuzzy heart did
Remember some words that do please.

A Bank Robber's Bad Luck With His Ex-Girlfriend

Such a delicious,
Warmed-over feeling
Prose set on paper can bring.
Eruptions of giggly,
Rose-blushy stealing,
Amiss pulsing, some smiling, and pings.

Your carriage surprise,
Emphatic-wise,
Your printed warmth and your kink,
One mere half of paper,
One witty love rapier,
Touched-where this woman doth think.

Your Tongue Quicks Me

Ads profess false, few monographs
Or texts refuse electric pulse
To chosen points along the length
Of body. Yet, stimulus earns
Its line from mental heritage.

The maidenhead of life, inlaid by skins
Of nerves, in vitro rests content as
Cranium treasure. Better
Aphrodisiacs still unfound,
Most nimble lovers caress ids.

We masturbate each other, touch
To tingle, stroking only thought.
Your tongue's firm tip massages, quicks
My memory while my wet lips
Bring ecstasy. Our nova's words.

So used to highlights at midday,
We often lack to understand
That others' sense of glass is gone
Along with pills and wine. Never
Reclaimed. Our pleasure's their mystery.

Fraternity Pin

A kiss,
Of gold and blue,
Inlaid with attachment,
Announces modestly to others,
Our set.

C'est L'Amour, N'est-ce Pas

C'est l'amour, n'est-ce pas?
Hot chirping, *coeurs de papiers*,
Bangles, gin-dashed pomegranate
Juice: *debauchees pari passu*.

Next door, nuptials *pari passu*
Picnic: shared ripe pomegranate
Seeds, exchanged c*oeurs de papiers*;
Valentines. *C'est l'amour, n'est-ce pas?*

Goldy and the Bear: A Modern *Cyrch a Chuta* for Two Brain-Fried Nerds

Goldilocks' imagined ballet,
Before stuffed teddies, swaying,
Black leather tights, while lying
Trust-up. My tongue adores days
Perfumed by your words. We display
Somatic affections, way-
Ward licks and lollies belie our contentions.
Our cerebral toys bounce; mental
Rustic joys train relays.

A Midsummer *Alcaics*

Your twilight sunshine happiness directed
Toward single, shady blossomless substance
Brings golden halos. Sometimes, given
"Merriment," projected, withstands monsoons.

I frequent sunfilled meadows (satisfied
By balmy climates, glistening galaxies
Spin, stellar commands issue), repose.
Relative atmosphere changes occur.

We create fragile traditions. Delicate
Bursts entwine. Somewhere, harmony's uncanny
Beat, captured, struggles; forcing flowers.
Galactic holiday ... beachless starshine.

Apple

Today I ate an apple.
Held it in my hand, really.
Thought of Italy and Spain,
Of you in golden sunlight. Delicious.
Crunches of hikes and cycling.
Cyprus trees garnering rounded corners.
Our loving beaches sounded waves,
Sunsets and linguini.
Abella Malus.
Campania.

KJ Hannah Greenberg

A Young Co-ed's Argonaut-Inspired Springtime Fancy

Above me grow the solemn hills of Phi.
Odd flowers bloom, weave variegated roads,
For nanny goats and butterflies to roam.

Beyond, like many stems, pillars arise,
Their pates adorned with ivory seals of state.
Below, ships shine, such tiny colored beads
Strung on a cord with earth and sky and hope.

Men make dreams; their hearts make talking trash.
But one low creature of the land holds fast.

Such minds may play like naughty Billy goats,
Spill visions of some golden, unsung lambs,
Whose fleece and tender ways suggest a smile;
Memories of a time that knew no name,
Still-folded, while upon the blushing land.

Joining

At our union,
Nature attended more than bloomed,
Pale vows connected us.

Gibbous Shoats and Other of Ardor's Follies

Gibbous Shoats, characterized by lunar convexity,
Ambled in the near light of an equinox's evening sun.
In close proximity, other critters, laboratory escapees, nightmares all,
Sauntered. Those roustabouts mewed, perplexed by certain mutterings
Spewing from imaginary hedgehogs plus fairly jaded fairies.

Animal pregnancies never before stymied this old agrarian as did those hybrids.
Coordinating their welfare sucked out all adequate energy since stable
Hands, farm wives, and assorted unskilled helpers ran; they eschew evil.
Even creative links to their grandparents' pasts or toward shared teachers' warnings
Issued small solace, so intent was their shunning of chimerae frolicking in moonlight.

Alone, I opposed windowsills, interior rooms, and meadows full of beings
Fashioned from crazy dreams, beheld best when captive. Emblematic,
Those wild mentations spun seismic upheavals of the intimate kind; gave reference
Regarding love's foibles, mistakes, regrettable moments. None
Faded. Confronted, they laughed their way to more mischievous follies.

My Boyfriend Coughs up Platitudes

My boyfriend coughs up platitudes.
His frenetically managed public statements,
Insinuate much about moderation's sensibilities,
As pertain to middle-aged matrons.
"Run," urge my friends, "return to service."

Elsewhere, the need for social change,
Sweetens days grown dusky with
"Read-to-me" stories meant for grownups.
Brief chapters were ne'er the province of women or tow heads.
"Quick," advises my family, "take cover."

At present, politics play heart chambers.
Philosophy's okay for classrooms, but
Road-ready rhetoric surpasses quips on the mat.
Loving needs be managed by words gently spoken.
"Abruptly," recommends my gut, "abandon this project."

HURT

Heart's Cry Bed: Recalibrating for the New Semester

My heart's cry bed, its cornerstone crafted
From motes malevolent, from games ill-drafted,
But played, repeatedly, among displaced victims
Their dogs, their cantaloupes,
Or other new-found vices.

Prison or party, rum shakes insides
Like business negotiated away, while astride
Deferences lingering on the edge;
Our mental refrigerators fill
With vast amounts of leafy greens.

False accusations, long seasons' worth,
Killed a clerk whose untimely berth
Positioned her against unnatural amounts
Of stuff employed to defeat
Cantankerous cardiovascular sickness.

Next September, let's not frolic,
Makes waves of enzymes anabolic,
Give no chest to chest efforts
Nor common medications' effect
On attentions misplaced by emotional defrauding.

Goldfish Hangover

Pillow. Parkway. Pillow. Parkway.
Gassed up, I motor
North for jobs or chump change.

One bleary eye,
I smile for classes,
Yesterday's Scotch and Soda,*
Left in glasses,
Alongside a friend.

Little aquatic, Mr. Gilded Gills,
Sagacious lord of clear utopia,
Your little fishy dance and
Forsaken silence spangled
All night.

Afterwards, I did not discharge,
Choosing, instead,
Asphyxiation,
On the alleged
Goodness of the invisible.

Our harmonic music vanquished,
I, too, am stilled.
You, an extension of my heart
Have been snuffed out
In a cocktail cup.

Scotch and Soda is the name of a drama association in Pittsburgh.

Trumpeters, Drummers, Dancers, plus Elephants: Princes' Promises

Imperfect sunsets, small ocean waves, empty beaches,
Plus a singular, beautiful horn,
Which, on a hash-induced lark, he purchased,
Proved my choice was right for me.

Squandering grand spans long ago ceased to fill
My best moments except to kill through hardy
Participation in mining fool's gold. I believe
Horses, wild banners, all merriment, ultimately gets manufactured.

This year's *topoi's rimmonim*,
Red, with abundant seeds of lassitude,
Listlessness enough for all manner of trumpeters,
Drummers, dancers, plus elephants.

So many sparkling smiles,
Mischievous as crocodile banquets,
Accompany each kerfuffle among the high bred.
Such that my small nephew's five fingered salute's all Arabic.

Entire societies will incinerate as long as we persist
In ignoring bacterial-strength bogus goodness.
Europe's memories and the New World's need reinforcement.
Princes' promises hold nothing.

KJ Hannah Greenberg

Poisoning via Toothbrush After "Romancing"

Across the plenty of Illinois, supernumerary measures safeguarded
My tank, my trunk, your overstuffed suitcase, my sort-of new laptop.
You named each crop, the parameters of their growth seasons, their pests.

Such credentialing in orchards, alongside this attention-starved mortal,
Necessarily pointed toward the fuzzy features we felled party night,
When I was shepherded athwart merry straits to your doyenne-like center.

Even now, I'm baffled that childish habits remain the basis of young bonding
Whether one's got sufficient resources to translate alphabets or simply vomits up
Precocious fantasies, recited slowly, verbatim, while cataloging toxins.

Since decreased cosmic energy reduces temperature, rainfall, nutrients,
Local avifauna and boys still find themselves driven to savagery;
Ordinary balustrades long ago yielded to our related, egregious posturing.

Recall, after one crooked baseball cap, approximately at sunrise, your beauty,
Bought for hoonage, also happy ego, plus another queen bee's mean rictus,
Strobed my mental alluvium long enough for you to hitch a ride.

Thus, some professor's only child, your basset, and your bass music,
Accompanied me toward bungalows mooring parking lots, lifted away
My flehmen response, caring neither that it was cued or hidden.

Surely amusement parks offer no comparatives to the sepulchral site I visited.
As always, my ordinary obeisance necessarily bent toward shiny things
When my talus stuck out far enough to kick at emotional schist, rococo talk.

Your tanzanite-colored sheath roofed no ablutions, offered little shelter
For eyes wide, hands splayed 'til rigid. Ohio's littoral on one side,
Walled in elsewise; no daddy-wrought capex could have hoped to cover you.

In sum, amontillado's great, but on the interstate, academic heiresses
Can't demand more than footnotes. You became wearing.
So I chose the salivating hound even as I applied borax to your toothbrush.

An *Ae Freislighe*: How to Get Your Girlfriend Pregnant

Matrimony' objective,
Versus sexual detours,
Teaches maidens selective
Schemes; i.e., chivalry's rescored.

"Potency means manliness,"
Quotes society. Esteem
Encourages randiness;
Experience ranks supreme.

Well done, human condition!
Pig-tails and jocks' affect
Stances for the best position.
(With traditional regrets.)

Graphic, Animated Features

He made no mention,
Intending, not at all,
To sell such singular
Life moments.

Yet, in movie houses' back rows,
He'd sworn more furry fiends
Than were displayed by the celluloid's
Graphic, animated features.

Apartment building basements, too,
Provided settings
Amiable to focused professing of
Assorted stray hairs and lipstick stains.

Those sorry choices,
Among piles of whites, cottons, delicates
Scooped, rose, flailed against
Her better sensibilities.

Such troubling mundanities,
When practiced in parked cars,
By him with others,
Resulted in births of absentee lovers.

Crocodile Tears

Silver fish, in silver pool,
Precious refracted light,
Heavenly sun jewel.

Murky mind, muddied might,
Clever reptile predator,
Deep bog blight.

Lightning flash.

Singular mortality.
The lily pads quiver.

Christina Rossetti's "Birthday" to a Satirical Beat*

My heart is like a singing bird,
Whose nest is in a desert bare.
My heart is like an apple tree,
Whose limbs are plucked and oversheared.
My heart is like a cracked snail's shell,
That rots beneath a brackish sea.
My heart is sadder than all these,
Because my love has come to me.

Raise me a platform of cotton rags,
Hang it with wolf skin and crocodiles.
Carve it in stone and lizards' toes,
Amid serpents and beetle eyes.
Work it in darkness and brittle twigs,
Work in gray mornings and blackened skies,
Because the low point of my life,
Has come, my love has come to me!

See Appendix for the original poem that inspired this.

Stained Sheets:
Some Emotional Hazards of Hooking Up

The first day,
After the rains stopped,
Your way was quick;
Felt like I'd been hit.

The second day,
Wet with your effort,
We laughed too loudly,
Rushing to replace the moment.

The third day,
I slept in.

The fourth day,
Your drank bourbon, neat,
Spilled ice on our sheets, vacated
Your eyes from the premises.

The fifth day,
Poetry flowed
Except when we snarled verses
Juxtaposed with silent resentment.

The sixth day,
We lacked time
For all but fast forward;
Windup monkeys do better.

Day seven's
Rest was relief;
Sombulence can reckon
Better than most intimacy.

Simple Arithmetic

Fleas please more than dogs
Hearing about giraffes necking
Together in zoos.

Gin and tonic, shaken,
Stirs up smoky whales of smiles
Since such pipes otherwise run cold.

Potato famines move towns
To new coasts, boating so many families away from children
That paternity suites refuse the penthouse.

I add your somatic discomfort to mine,
Subtract a bit for garden-type apprehension,
Then multiple by identifiable stimuli.

Perhaps general mood states ought
To trickle down the hippocampal more often.
Meanwhile, there's chocolate doughnuts.

Trees at Sunset

Along the way, trees,
Such large paper doilies,
Black against the hillside,
In stenciled pride,
Mark double patterns.

Some silhouettes,
Next to life's blue paper,
Contrast better in dim moments,
Than during entire days' worth of splendor.

Morning's league lacks sure perspicuity.

Sentiment's Chowder

Long distance lovers, all
Doilies and belvederes,
Like sweet, European fish
Served with ketchup.

Local friends, in contrast,
Accept stewed heads,
Braised flanks,
Sometimes even sentiment's chowder.

While the Dew Coughed

While the dew coughed
Up many promises
Exhaling, until evaporation
Desires, droplet-sized,

His tractor tore swatches
Ripped neat rows of moisture,
Mowed, and otherwise raked,
Hope into piles,

In some boudoirs,
Lavender's a weed
Thistle conjures no medicinal richness,
Boxwood's unknown.

Those sites find marigold grace,
In municipal dividers, and
Welfare in yellowed wallpaper,
Whose printed roses affix even tiles.

Quinoa in My Keyboard and Other Traces of Fantasy

Puffed cereal sticks
Both escape and delete
When prototype verse
Competes with sombulence.

I'd rather hug a porcupine
Than sell even one of your
Motes, pages, or letters,
On eBay.

Your sentiments,
Shared,
Like yesterday's windup bears,
Remain publicly immaterial.

Our union'd be copacetic,
Glamoured in good wishes,
And otherwise kind of sparkly
If only you'd appear.

Small Payment for a Protracted Span

Maidenhood's a small payment for a protracted span of sartorial retribution.
Until next season, anyway, prints featuring fields or woods will
Be so completely eclipsed by snowflake patterns that fabric stressing forbs,
Whether needle, bract, or foliole, might be, perhaps, better served in stagnate pools.

Such vigor as communal suppers deal, less their ergotic mistakes,
Seem scant remuneration for feeding crowds mind-numbing wastes of time.
Stewards of such events contend, incessantly, that fixations with compelling thoughts
Leave kitchens covered in grease or overwrought by mummified hamsters.

It's nice to acquiesce to those with whom we share the future, yet
That energy remains the province of goodwives needing sugar cubes, not bitters.
For all intents and purposes, cultivating bonds means moving past regrets,
Indicating who is and who's not dancing alongside of imperfectly sprung witnesses.

KJ Hannah Greenberg

Deviating Under Starlight: Whispers of Divestment

I'm deviating left and right,
In the sun, plus twice at night.
Might as well feign like Clytie;
When running versus the starlight.

True, no nymph or maiden fair,
Cares like me about how near
Your breath vibrates or how you swear
To liberate ones whom you "hold dear."

If only chains, which confine souls,
Could mold our wants, change what we know,
Then cosmic dramas might unfold
Regret's roots when like this behold.

Until that hour, until that chime, I
Meander oddly through this clime,
Roaming intentions, roving design,
I'm diverging from our union, meantime.

HIGHWAYS

A Bank Robber's Bad Luck With His Ex-Girlfriend

Decided

My knight in armor will arrive,
Upon his steadfast steed.
Along the way, he'll race the wind,
Assuredly, he'll lead.

When he will then dismount to earth,
I'll view him from my sill.
That quaint young man of noble birth,
I do adore him still.

Except, I've spent a lot of time, lately, in the city
Vacationing away from honeysuckle glens, good witches, and crystal ponds.
Gem-colored fish mean scat when compared to my boys at the bar.
Pastel creatures, all finery, manners, plus little else, bore me, excluding graffiti.
Disband hairy giants' collectives! Burn sun-blessed veldts! Explode dwarf-sized despots!
I'd no more hook up with a would-be ruler than with a bout of melanoma.

If I descended my circled stair,
To walk upon the land,
He'd greet me there, about midway,
His glove beneath my hand.

Near my manor lord's paths we'd stroll,
A pair of friends from olde.
The forbs would brush our youthful legs,
Until the guy got bold.

Nah, not interested. Fairytale endings rot for princesses.
There's no use being inscribed, as exemplary, for perpetuity,
Immobilized behind briars, in a tower, or under a spell.
Dry lips, peeling skin; that's the stuff of harpies. I'm modern.
Better to sling a few fire bolts, extend greetings with my crossbow,
Indicate clearly I'm no incompetent. Buffoonery's for jesters, not uptown girls.

Colluvium

Many guffaws later, I pressed your memory
Onto electronic pages where a controlling nature, as well as all
Other manners of accretions mattered little.

Moreauvia's beauties, thereafter, colored by screed, plus misanthropy
Gone wrong, sang ballads filled with fish sucking away at plankton,
Also, billies chewing fence posts past familiar muster.

Such rhetorical geeps and their kindred small fry make good fodder;
Gossips, though, rot as bedmates. I'd rather sip sassafras from a chipped cup.
There's negligible good stone-like mementos and nothing like collected blips.

My Chemistry Class

My chemistry class, high on gender pH equivalents of red
Cabbage, found that familiar solutions enchant avenues for combustion.
Noble patience, fursuits, fruity candy, extra piercings,
Even wayward deposits of chapattis, otherwise meant to spoon with Petri
Dishes, begged better wisdom.

Love's fonts, as colored by redox reactions, like lapidaries' stones,
Tumble big and bright, bring fug-filled beakers, wide vials
Overflowing with viscous emulsions, plus occasional, solidified,
Hope. Such substances, far sexier than simples, greet or cheat
Adolescents; historically, kids will work the bench until lunchtime.

Play-yard bullies, brainiacs, football brawn equally admitted that radio
Waves, hence directed, remained unable to fuse intellectual panache/teenage initiative.
Until doxies, formaldehyde-based, otherwise centrifuged, force eyelash waste
Off of maps of fractured elements, forgetting would take too long to merit
Further spectrophotoic segregations of men from boys.

Droving Last Year's Love

Moving from place to place,
Grazing by beastly means,
Upon innocence's demands
For face work.

Our ghastly talks idle,
Bringing tears, evoking hearts' labor.
Until such efforts morph deeply
As gaucho stew.

Working dogs, some supervising flocks,
Look askance;
They're accustomed to corralling
Like-minded critters.

Lassos, packhorses, all mechanisms,
Plus lowing stock,
Aid in feeding, mating, sleeping,
When ushering in fancies.

After all, mustering's a long job.
It's difficult for herdboys, manhood blooming
Close to nightclub indulgences,
To understand.

Fire Song

White wisps, blue tendrils,
Flame yellow kissed
Jewelweed bursts,
Red starred hearts,
Warm, then wane.

Wafting past earthen lances
Advancing only to sing
Where death wrings
Woodland mysteries.

Besot by unplanned grandeur,
Mysteries of blessing
Evade touch and thought,
Mimicking worse moments.

Birds nest where lives,
Beaten down, slip
Alone among reserves.
Temple records, only,
Remember our remorse.

Ephemerids

Ms. Alfred, Buffaloberry's cat,
Can be relied upon to be limp,
Joking all the while
About being "a Jewish Mother."

Feline helpings of soup,
Chicken, vegetables, bread,
Plied upon unsuspecting guests
Otherwise sate most comers.

Heaping plates hold,
Steamed plus boiled delicacies,
Morph prey species into
Vapid volunteers, who fill bellies.

Jewels, travels, plus dead animals' skins
Evoke an unwillingness to study law,
Practice medicine, or remain all but
Barren per competitive careers.

Provisional divisions evolve
Beyond familiar tails, pointy ears,
Sharp responses or soothed consciousness;
Prefabricated intellectual submission delights.

A Bank Robber's Bad Luck With His Ex-Girlfriend

Hence, it's familial feline stuff
That attends weddings, graduations, other
Celebrations decked in gender-bias'
Soft ego touch.

Courting men means bothering
Among electronic appliances,
Land grant universities,
And answering machines.

Better to flick wet tissues,
Their wadded hillocks covering carpets,
Than to clamor, a loud,
About social justice.

As a result, it's small wonder
When domesticated fry distance
Themselves from norms, paw-sing,
All the while, to accommodate cultural nuances.

Your Knees Remain Extant:
Deriding an Internet Hussy

Dandyism, even mere contemporary jackanapery,
Makes homage possible, daily, to the likes of you,
A species redolent of more than common cleavage.

No altricial chick, your profligated flesh compares to sour laundry,
Why pretend to hide your precious sacristy, to be underimpressed
With people commandeering window offices or crenellated opinions?

Hug-seeking husbands, missing notice, and youths wanting "motherly" adorations,
All leave fresh trails of litter streaming from your technological kitty box,
Where neither kanga nor fitted skirt cover your most important portcullis.

No known palliative cures such habit, turns dyscrases into moral abattoirs,
Otherwise exchanges totipotent behaviors for epicene moves.
Destiny declares, instead, that your knees will remain extant on the Internet.

A Bank Robber's Bad Luck With His Ex-Girlfriend

His Mistresses' Grandeur
Astride Common Sense

Without kon-tiki platters, braced to receive select sorts of meerschaum, during big events,
Those vacuous strata, represented by better dressed women, deflate, drop all
Pretensions of *droit du seigneur*, elect, instead to sucker punch would-be plaintiffs.

It seems that in places where competition's rife with gabbling, where fishes fly or not
Depending on rhymed compensation, which often gets pushed past bezoars, other blather,
Ambitious persons swell, high aspirations aflutter until met with impassable strictures.

Consequent to such impenetrable gasping, those most talented protagonists,
Hands behind heads, barking until gorged, go all kissy face, forgive,
Take fresh bribes, march back for unsullied clothes, then express readiness to renew.

After supplementary vows, they employ their special silviculture for making whoopee,
Also, for facilitating equals to basic telephony; the king wakes by drum beat,
Orders an execution or six, embezzles a cool half billion, then naps.

The value of such goings on makes for stabile memories, conjured sledges or rushes,
Predictable market conditions. What's more, estivation, the likes of which
Embrace snow, not sun, enjoys precipitation. Life's best bits are necessarily juicy.

Pausing From Eating Shelducks

He had rationalized, stooped to claim, from his nadir,
Of sebum, plus tight, ill-fitting necktie,
That salvation can arrive only when
Guns, good looks, other circumstantial evidence become null,
Void, in bedrooms, barrooms, also playgrounds.

I paused from eating shelducks to volley;
Old satiations move the way of inventoried ills.
Social armadas are not wont to voluntarily
Atone, amend, otherwise apologize,
Make good on chits owed, unless provoked.

In answer, he coughed, salivated a bit,
Said that cultural bonfires mean nothing
Juxtaposed to trapped thalamic agencies
As possessed by petulant hedgehogs;
Spiny mammals tend to grunt, snuffle, or squeak displeasure.

For closure, I proposed he stymie certain engines.
Select machines' meretricious clogs entrammel,
Bring to the fore disfigured social matters, smoke, mirrors,
Solve naught; just roll credits.

Some Cowboys

Some cowboys,
(All yippee-i-o,
Plus Southern Comfort
Decked out in bull paddles)
Join Rodeos

After their mounts
(Shamed before seventy,
Hobbled from hoofing,
Retreated for ice packs)
Toss them.

Such rebels sit pretty
(Chiseled determination notwithstanding,
Dreaming of morphing
Their rides into hamburger)
While selling car insurance.

Among Bungalows

Among bungalows, irascible hedgehogs dance,
Prancing among moonbeam colors when otherwise not bouncing
Along improvident garden paths, in search of moths, good wine, illicit love.

Such sedge beasts believe their beauty is façade enough
Both for pounding on slick, slate lanes and for engaging in private pastimes.
(They're sincere, albeit, in their sharing of glazed galettes, good brandy, thin cigars).

Our plinths, in contrast, seem to rest on relatively uncertain rock;
People gyre like sloths, all tiny ears, slow changes, claws,
While awaiting evolution's gift of boggart ways.

Until skipping comes naturally, we two footers remain mere students of midnight
Rheology, as learned from unfortunate heights, constrained by citified
Compunctions, familial fashions, regular embarrassments.

We've yet to embrace the varied manners of predation used by flower bed culprits,
Their friends, some cousins, along with creatures grown by maddened writers;
Human frolicking don't flow easily.

When Lowing Wisents Agitate

School marms' meetings blossom nonce, also disappear,
While lowing wisents agitate among cornflowers, all blue, bright, cheery.
Even the most cowed matrons find reasons to sometimes kick catalysts into overdrive,
Given handsome cowboys. Kernels do occasionally pop on the stalk.

Old maids, it seems, have little interest in evoking the specters of dating
When there exist towns, cities, plus select trailer parks, full of studly others.
Rumor claims they'll go half way to the moon with pensioners,
Rather than bother spelling out plays to fumbling youths.

Such "wild gals," after all, come in sizes, colors, ages banned from centerfolds,
Hence, their songs ring much sweeter compared to those of airbrushed beauties.
Crones appreciate flaccid arms, rotund bellies, bewhiskered jaws, occasional indigestion.
As unguent, they serve by fastening more than mid America's pants.

Reciprocity

When his mother's intubation ended,
Her tumors having prized away
All nature of recognizable personality,
I brought him meatloaf.

He remained positioned bedside,
Learning nurses' names
And doctors' temperaments.
The next paper sack contained underwear.

Hope climbed those walls
As effectively as he had earlier leapt
Relationship quicksand.
No laptop battery was forgotten.

If she had been consumed
By chimera, warring hedgehogs, or
Ravenous lions,
I'd have ported him no paperbacks.

As it were, her IVs flowered
Until she flatlined.
Crying and howling,
He marked our last part of sharing.

Three Pillows

You shift, nudging batting toward my chin,
Your arm sways near my shoulder,
Pulling blanket from my middle.

I snuggle, warm, immobile, comforted,
Familiar breathing wafts my ear,
Spicy aroma of our shared dinner.

Once more, a bolster slips beneath my knees.
You nestle your head on my softness,
Insisting I'm your cushion, your satisfaction.

Rearranging my neck, I lift,
Spy over our covers, seek
Whether or not you're tucked.

Volleying back our linen surplus, I
Will your lids shut, your respiration calm.
I wish sleep to descend upon you.

Yet, you stir once and again.
Meanwhile, I count our altruistic movements;
There's three pillows plus us.

Practiced at sharing, we generate extra.
I reach gently, place two bolsters floorward.
Then we sleep.

Ready to Synchronize

I'm ready to synchronize
Entire orchestras of starfish wanting
To blend waves of animal mortality
With crystalline victory's consigned
Ardor.

These lived elusive times,
Our spans' derived depths of brine,
Tear lakes together in puddles,
So magnificent as their aquatic flowers blooming
Beneath.

Only so many meteors might fall
Until the ocean belches
More that it whispers
When waved winds acquire
Depth.

Chance's don reigns o'er white seahorses,
Shape-shifters, meant to tweak convention,
To distress the requiem
Of shadowy literary forms
Forever.

Emotional Kerfuffles:
Second Unions

Pages turn away from extraneous, extra, additional, unnecessary verbiage.
Unless a scout's trained in chemistry.
Such a desirable, conservative flair is sought
For traditional weddings.
The radical life supersedes only thereafter.

At those junctures, security promised by dint of stance, words, or alternatives, flees.
Entire emotional kerfuffles ensue
Consisting of unconscionable social
Doodles and many unhappy events.
Only years later will a bride realize her fortune.

Experienced in too many like vistas, situations, experiences and kindred moments,
An old-timer, stuffed with clay, dryer than leather,
Ceased sacrificing moisture;
He had already stopped shrinking,
Failing repeatedly, he knew, was a means of ascension.

His jilted woman, angry, combo killer, huntress, wicked crone, met the geezer.
Such unions, hardly novel in their occurrence,
Happened anyway.
Glazeware fired twice or so remains resilient to all but breakage
They live carefully ever after.

KJ Hannah Greenberg

Conclusion: Hurt Is to Healing

Streaks of lightning, skyward fires,
Dawn's misty clouds, sunshine's stars,
Flaming rivers, pulling us higher,
Praise horizon line.

Desert-blown winds, desert-blown gore,
Sands of the nations, blood of the war,
Tear stained legions, living out lore,
Praise horizon line.

Herbs' healing blossoms, folks' fostered kin,
Rainbows' bright endings, storms' slow begin,
Forces felt human, forces within,
Praise horizon line.

Death, birth and passage, eternal clash,
Mixture of history, horrid morass,
Victory's prices, expensive peace,
Praise horizon line.

Sleep while the wind sleeps, rest with the sky,
Danger in fire, safe while it's nigh,
Wheels on life's river, breath whispers by,
Praise horizon line.

Bloom tiny babies, bring woolly sheep,
Light scented torches, oils to seep,
Shadows encroach here,
Truth leaves us peace,
Praise horizon line.

Hurt is to healing, blood is to tears,
Laughter takes illness, songs rout out fears,
Living brings losses, living repairs,
Living repairs.

APPENDIX

A Birthday
By Christina Rossetti

My heart is like a singing bird
      Whose nest is in a water'd shoot;
My heart is like an apple-tree
      Whose boughs are bent with thickset fruit;
My heart is like a rainbow shell
      That paddles in a halcyon sea;
My heart is gladder than all these
      Because my love is come to me.

Raise me a dais of silk and down;
      Hang it with vair and purple dyes;
Carve it in doves and pomegranates,
      And peacocks with a hundred eyes;
Work it in gold and silver grapes,
      In leaves and silver fleurs-de-lys;
Because the birthday of my life
      Is come, my love is come to me.

First published in *Macmillan's Magazine*, vol iii, Feb 1861, p 325; reprinted in *Goblin Market, and Other Poems*, Macmillan & Co, Cambridge, 1862, p56.

A Bank Robber's Bad Luck With His Ex-Girlfriend

KJ Hannah Greenberg gave up all manner of academic hoopla to chase imaginary hedgehogs and to raise children. After almost two decades of belly dancing, home birthing, herbal medicine making, and occasional basket weaving, she dusted off her keyboard and began to churn out smoothies, vegetable soup, and more creative work than might be considered proper for a middle-aged woman. To date, dozens of venues, including *BRICKrhetoric, Ken* Again, Language and Culture Magazine, Mad Swirl, Poetica Magazine, Poetry Super Highway, The New Vilna Review, Unfettered Verse,* and *vox poetica*, have published Hannah's poetry.

Meanwhile, Hannah formed Expressedly Yours Writing Workshops, took on editorial responsibilities at publications hither and yon, and was twice nominated for the Pushcart Prize. She established a matchmaking service for words such as "twaddle" and "xylophone," too.

Incorrigible at a molecular level, Hannah continues to write across genres. Look for her fiction in forums ranging from *Bewildering Stories, Fiction365, Morpheus Tales,* and *Weirdyear* to *Bartleby Snopes*, MENSA's *Calliope,* and the *Journal of Microliterature*. Also, consider buying Hannah's collection of light essays, *Oblivious to the Obvious: Wishfully Mindful Parenting* and her scholarly *Conversations on Communications Ethics*. What's more, an assemblage of her flash and short stories, *Don't Pet the Sweaty Things*, will be available in 2012.

Publication Credits

"A Special Dance," *Gypsy Daughter's Brown Bagazine*.

"A Young Co-ed's Argonaut-Inspired Springtime Fancy," *The Camel Saloon*, Jan 2011.

"An *Ae Freislighe*: How to Get Your Girlfriend Pregnant," *Poetry Super Highway*, Mar 2009.

"C'est L'Amour, N'est-ce pas," *Getting Something Read*, Jun 2009.

"Christina Rossetti's 'Birthday' to a Satirical Beat," *Unfettered Verse*, Dec 2008.

"Crocodile Tears," *The New Aesthetic*, Feb 2011.

"Decided," *Moon Drenched Fables*, Mar 2011.

"Deviating Under Starlight: Whispers of Divestment," *vox poetica*, Nov 2010.

"Droving Last Year's Love," *Danse Macabre Belles Lettres*, Apr 2010.

"Emotional Kerfuffles: Second Unions," *Cantaraville*, Oct 2009, 172-173.

"Engineering Wizards' Best and Last (Interstate Enchantment)," *The Shine Journal*, Mar 2011.

"Ephemerids," *Ragazine*, Oct 2010.

"Fire Song," *Callused Hands*, Nov 2009.

"Fraternity Pin," *Unfettered Verse*, Oct 2008.

"Friendsake," *The Cat's Meow*, Sep 2010.

"Gibbous Shoats and Other of Ardor's Follies," *Stride Magazine*, Nov 2009.

"Goldfish Hangover," *The Greensilk Journal*, Nov 2009.

"Heart's Cry Bed: Recalibrating for the New Semester," *Social-i Magazine*, Dec 2010.

"His Mistresses' Grandeur Astride Common Sense." *BRICKrhetoric*, May 2011.

"Hurt Is to Healing," *Joyful!* Sep 2008.

"Joining," *vox poetica*, Sep 19, 2011.

"My Boyfriend Coughs up Platitudes," *vox poetica*, Jan 2010.

"My Chemistry Class," *Lesser Flamingo*, Mar 2010.

"Quinoa in My Keyboard and Other Traces of Fantasy," *BRICKrhetoric*, May 2011.

"Ready to Synchronize," *Whispers From the Unseen*, May 2009.

"Sentiment's Chowder," *vox poetica*, Feb 2010.

"Small Payment for a Protracted Span," *Social-i Magazine*, Dec 2010.

"Stained Sheets: Some Emotional Hazards of Hooking Up," *Palehouse*, Dec 2009.

"Three Pillows," *Fallopian Falafel*, Feb 2011.

"Trees at Sunset," *vox poetica*, Aug 2011.

"Trumpeters, Drummers, Dancers, plus Elephants: Prince's Promises," *Fallopian Falafel*, Jun 2011.

"While the Dew Coughed," *The Lesser Flamingo*, Mar 2010.

"Your Knees Remain Extant: Deriding an Internet Hussy," *Bewildering Stories*, Jun 2011.

"Your Tongue Quicks Me," *Sheepshead Review*, Dec 2010.

www.ingramcontent.com/pod-product-compliance
Lightning Source LLC
Chambersburg PA
CBHW070102100426
42743CB00012B/2637